PAMPHLETS ON AMERICAN WRITERS · NUMBER 71

UNIVERSITY OF MINNESOTA

Van Wyck Brooks

BY WILLIAM WASSERSTROM

UNIVERSITY OF MINNESOTA PRESS · MINNEAPOLIS

Printed in the United States of America at
the North Central Publishing Co., St. Paul

Library of Congress Catalog Card Number: 68-64754

PUBLISHED IN GREAT BRITAIN, INDIA, AND PAKISTAN BY THE OXFORD
UNIVERSITY PRESS, LONDON, BOMBAY, AND KARACHI, AND IN CANADA
BY THE COPP CLARK PUBLISHING CO. LIMITED, TORONTO

To my sister, Sylvia

WILLIAM WASSERSTROM, who has written or edited five books, chiefly on modern American and European literature, is a professor of English at Syracuse University. Among his books are *Heiress of All the Ages, The Time of the Dial,* and *Civil Liberties and the Arts.*

⤳ Van Wyck Brooks

THE displacement of Van Wyck Brooks from the center to the farthest margins of literary influence today is surely a stunning shift of taste. In 1920 Brooks was regarded as the undisputed heir of the great tradition in American thought — the radical, reformist, prophetic, "organic" tradition which adopted Emerson as its source of inspiration, took *The American Scholar* as its point of departure, and envisioned as its point of terminus a civilization in which the creative spirit, in all its social and imaginative forms, might flourish. To this old enterprise Brooks had brought intransigent zeal and incomparable flair — a genius for clarifying thought, said his comrade-at-arms on *The Seven Arts*, James Oppenheim. Today, Brooks's sovereign role in the transmission of this classic American tradition, his *oeuvre* of inquiry into its bearing on modern letters in America, is either ignored or disdained.

"The most interesting American books," Richard Poirier observes in his presumably definitive study of this tradition, *A World Elsewhere* (1966), "are an image of the creation of America itself, of the effort, in the words of Emerson's Orphic poet, to 'Build therefore your own world.'" For reasons of ignorance or disdain, I guess, Poirier excludes Brooks from his study — even though Brooks had acquired, a half-century ago, an international fame and following as the leading spokesman for Emerson's idea, as a most compelling opponent of those younger writers who decided that American genius could flourish only outside the United States. At first he shared their view. But eventually he came to think that America, by virtue of its history and ideology, was not only itself the very emblem of the creative

5

life but was, too, the best place on earth to locate the republic of letters. And he composed a series of books which monumentalized Emerson's Orphic vision. Suddenly, when his art had achieved certain marvels of transformation, he lost voice, heart, taste, courage for the task. Somehow he lost the thread of his own passion and found himself in an abyss of his own devising. A really major figure in the seedtime of modern thought, he became a minor figure in the time of efflorescence — victim of the very forces he had discerned, named, and condemned. Although he turned out to be a critic of divided mind, a man whose life was broken in half, in one respect his career was all of a piece: from first to last he sought to transform America from an industrial jungle into a place fit for the realization of Emerson's Romantic dream.

There was no sign of faltering will in those early books, published between 1908 and 1925, which introduced a prodigy endowed with audacity of learning, fluency of speech, an apparent assurance of mind, and a cosmopolitan experience unmatched in American criticism of that day. Born in Plainfield, New Jersey, in 1886, educated there and in Europe where his family had spent a year in 1898, Brooks had entered Harvard in 1904. Completing work for his degree a year early, in 1907, he had gone on a second European journey, to England, where for eighteen months he had lived as a free-lance journalist and where he had written and published *The Wine of the Puritans* in 1908. He came back to New York that year and remained until 1911 when he went to California. There he married Eleanor Kenyon Stimson, whom he had known as a friend of childhood and youth and whose own life, both before and after Wellesley, had been spent going back and forth from Europe: "we were both in love with Europe and always had been."

Returning to England in 1913 with his new family — a son had

been born in 1912 — Brooks published the work written during
his California years, *The Malady of the Ideal.* This and *The
Wine of the Puritans* make a pair quite as the next pair, *John
Addington Symonds: A Biographical Study* (1914) and *The
World of H. G. Wells* (1914), were conceived and composed in
concert. The four, taken together, provide initial statements of
those ideas, passionately held, which were to shape Brooks's cri-
tique of and program for America in the celebrated essays, *America's Coming-of-Age* (1915) and *Letters and Leadership* (1918),
and the psychological studies, *The Ordeal of Mark Twain* (1920)
and *The Pilgrimage of Henry James* (1925). In these eight inter-
connected pieces of work, representing nearly two decades of
resolute and concentrated labor, Brooks focused his whole en-
ergy on a single theme. He sought to penetrate the conditions
which devastate and to disclose the environments which nurture
the springs of art in Europe and the United States.

I speak of these intricate things as if there is no problem in
reducing a thousand pages of intense prose — and hundreds of
pages of criticism of Brooks's prose — to a simple formula. But
the very resourcefulness of Brooks's mind and the opulence of
comment on Brooks's books have obscured certain obvious mat-
ters about which it is, at this late stage of judgment, no great
task to be forthright. Indeed, a certain likeness from book to book
has always been fairly plain. Stanley Edgar Hyman, for example,
describing Brooks's distinction between the actual "wine" of the
Puritans and the "aroma" of wine, recognized in this play of
metaphor an embryonic version of those distinctions between
highbrow and lowbrow on which Brooks was to build the myth
of America's coming of age. If you read backwards from lowbrow you discover Brooks maintaining that it was the Puritans'
taste for the material life of the New World which led in later
centuries to a sheer and bald commercialism: "wine." Read back-

7

wards from highbrow and you find Brooks arguing that it was the Puritans' simultaneous joy in the "aroma of the wine, the emphasis on the ideal, which became transcendentalism." The essential questions raised in *The Wine of the Puritans*, then, introduced a perplexity which was ever to vex Brooks, a man who retained all his life the habit of formulating modern questions in an archaic language. If art is defined as the Soul's perception of the Ideal, how can art enrich a society which was itself created out of a breach between Soul and Body, between Ideal and Real? Could America be made into a place where the life of thought and the life of action might be reconciled?

These were the lofty problems, invariably cast into pairs of metaphor, which led Brooks in *The Malady of the Ideal* to contrast the temper of German thought with the French. The French temperament, fixed firmly in the real world and engaged by the problems of social order, he called *rhetorical*. In contrast, the German mind, concerned with "truth, good, and beauty," the realm of the Ideal, was *poetical* in its drift. The true poet, rooted in the Real, fixed his attention unwaveringly on the Ideal and became therefore a great source of reconciliation, a visionary of order on earth. A rhetorician, however, was committed to the study of exterior consistency alone. "He takes his point of departure from an idea which in its primitive form is a sincere expression of himself. The next day looking deeper he perhaps discovers a new idea that cuts away the ground from under his former idea. But he is a practical man — he . . . therefore forces a consistency between the two ideas." As the circle of his thought arcs farther and farther away from that first, genuine perception, finally "he achieves a logical consistency; his work has a compact, finished quality. But where is truth?" Illustrating the practical effects of his theory, Brooks referred to Senancour and Maurice de Guérin, and arrived at last at Amiel, "true child of Geneva,"

8

in whom French and German influence came to a standoff, a sterile, immobilizing "fatal mixture of the blood." Neither German enough, "foolhardy" enough, to trust in intuition, nor French enough, rhetorical enough, to rely on disciplined rationalism, Amiel sat "like a spider in a kind of cosmic web spun from his own body, unable to find himself because he could not lose himself."

Before long, as we shall see, Brooks himself was to arrive at the condition in which *The Malady of the Ideal* leaves Amiel. Ironically, too, his next books, on Symonds and Wells, mark the emergence of Brooks the rhetorician, the practical critic whose work was compact and self-contained and consistent but — said his critics — Where was truth?

A disappointing book to read in 1914, the study of Symonds is an especially rewarding book to read now. For Brooks was only superficially preoccupied with his ostensible subject and was deeply engaged inquiring into his essential subject — himself. In its tiniest detail and in the sweep of its theme, the biography of Symonds is a clairvoyant essay in self-appraisal and self-revelation. Taking up the subject of his *Malady*, applying its theoretical system to English letters, Brooks presents Symonds as a victim of neuroticism so acute as to render him blind to the distinctions between "mundane and visionary values," between Real and Ideal. Symonds to his credit possessed a visionary mind; to his discredit, so Brooks believed, he was incapable of bearing the cost of vision and he turned instead to rhetoric, to the study of the humdrum. In order to support this reading, Brooks adopted a strategy which led him away from the ordinary pursuits of literary criticism and plunged him into the first of his exercises in the psychology of failure, the sociology of despair. Whatever else must be said, it cannot be gainsaid that this was pioneer work of a most taxing kind. And what has hitherto been left un-

9

said about Brooks is that his pioneering studies in literary psychology were informed by his reading in a single source, Bernard Hart's *The Psychology of Insanity*. This famous handbook was first published in England in 1912, shortly before Brooks's third European and second English sojourn in 1913. As he later told Robert Spiller — who repeated the anecdote to me — Hart's little book represented all that he knew of psychoanalysis. Whether or not he read Freud or Jung too, whom he mentions in print now and then, is uncertain. But there is no mention of Hart's work in Brooks's writing — a strange omission in the light of his remark to Spiller.

The Psychology of Insanity is a historic work. It is the first essay, both technical and lucid, which incorporates Freud's views on the general subject. This book, Hart wrote, "does not really occupy any definite place in the direct line of Freudian history, but is at once narrower and wider in its aim." It is narrower in that it deals with certain selected aspects of Freud's thought (Hart adopted the unconscious and the concept of repression but rejected Freud's views on sex) and it is wider "in that it attempts to bring those aspects into relation with lines of advance followed by other investigators." In its own right a remarkably sage and balanced essay, it is typical of its period, too, in its tone of wonder and certainty — wonder that some classic riddles of the psyche had been solved at last, certainty that some tentative propositions would turn out dogmatic truth.

In Hart's habit of discovering simple trauma behind complicated events, Brooks found sanction to support his own custom of searching out a "causal complex" which would simply explain everything. As applied to Symonds, this habit led Brooks to ascribe neurotic failure to a state of war between reason and action, passion and thought. Symonds' thought could not satisfy appetites generated by Symonds' passions; nor could Symonds, for reasons of health and "conscience," translate thought into action: "it was this complex [which] remained with him to the last" and ended ultimately in breakdown. Upon recovery, he discovered Whitman and through Whitman acquired "a lusty contempt for purely intellectual processes." Symonds struck a bad bargain with his instincts, Brooks said, and in consequence was transformed into a "congested poet" and *vulgariseur*, a maker of scholarly books which struggled to do what "only poetry can do" and are therefore best described as "high fantasy" not high accomplishment in humane letters.

Reading this comment on Symonds, anyone with even the skimpiest knowledge of Brooks's career must recognize in the pattern Brooks ascribes to Symonds' life the very pattern which best describes Brooks's life — including the rediscovery of Whitman. If I seem to be forcing a consistency where there is resemblance alone, Brooks's peroration dispels all doubt. The portrait of Symonds, chronology altered but otherwise changed only to include metaphoric rather than literal detail, could stand as a self-portrait: "Neurotic from birth, suppressed and misdirected in education, turned by early environment and by natural affinity into certain intellectual and spiritual channels, pressed into speculation by dogmatic surroundings and aesthetic study, his naturally febrile constitution shattered by over-stimulation, by wanting vitality denied robust creation, by disease made a wanderer, by disease and wandering together aroused to an unending, fretful activity — the inner history of Symonds could be detailed and charted scientifically."

After completing this book and publishing it in 1913–14, along with *The Malady of the Ideal* and *The World of H. G. Wells*, Brooks left England once again for New York. This time, however, the decision to return signified at last an end to wandering, an end to the disease of indecision which had plagued him since his departure from Harvard. Brooks's wanderings during this period of his life are not just of documentary interest. Nor do these represent mere sprightliness of curiosity on the part of a provincial bright young man. It is a rather more radical thing. For it was during these half-dozen years of inquiry into and contrast of certain American and European styles of life that Brooks cast about for reasons why he should remain at home or return abroad to live in determined rather than tentative exile. In these early works he sought to resolve a disquietude more pressing than troubled Amiel or Symonds. It is useful, therefore, to present a detailed chart of the inner history of Brooks's mind at the moment when he achieved his greatest fame and widest influence.

A "wanderer, the child of some nation yet unborn, smitten with an inappeasable nostalgia for the Beloved Community on the far side of socialism, he carried with him the intoxicating air of that community, the mysterious aroma of its works and ways." These are Brooks's words, written in eulogy to his beloved friend Randolph Bourne. But again biography and autobiography fuse: the sketch of Bourne is also a work of self-portraiture which intimates the state of Brooks's mind in the period beginning in 1914. Completing the book on Wells, whom he called a man of "planetary imagination," an "artist of society," Brooks convinced himself that America was ripe for rebirth on the far side of socialism. Smitten with an inappeasable nostalgia for utopia, he convinced himself, too, that a socialist America would be the place in which the life of the mind (the realm of the Ideal) and the life of action (the Real) might be brought to equilibrium. America, he said, was H. G. Wells "writ large."

Brooks at mid-decade was by no means a man of composed mind but was instead a man of divided will: the chief obsession of his divided mind was Europe. This obsession he shared, strangely, with the man he most despised, T. S. Eliot. To say that Brooks despised Eliot is no exaggeration. Although his published comment is restrained, his private comment, particularly in the later days of fascism, exhibits a barely controlled revulsion. The "Elioteers" are almost as bad as the Germans, he blurted in a letter (November 1941), to Bliss Perry. Brooks was peculiarly fierce not just because he despised Eliot's ideas but because, deep down, he shared Eliot's taste for the well-upholstered life of a European man of letters.

In Brooks's instance and Eliot's, in Pound's and Conrad Aiken's, John Gould Fletcher's and H. D.'s — that first wave of expatriate American writers — the dream of literature was inextricable from the dream of Europe. In the world Brooks knew as a child, that well-heeled and well-placed society of the eastern seaboard, Henry Adams' world, "a voyage to Europe was the panacea for every known illness and discontent." Unlike his compatriots who had few second thoughts about cloaking themselves in the "iridescent fabric" of Europe, Brooks was deeply torn. The causes of conflict lay in the special circumstances of his early life, that family life which was at once in harmony and in conflict with the Harvard cult of Europe, incarnate in Santayana. Why am I abroad, he had forced himself to think in 1908, when I believe in living at home? Part of the answer was by no means complicated — though it did involve some complications within his family. He was determined to escape Plainfield, New Jersey, and to avoid the "sadness and wreckage" which diminished the lives of his father and brother. In that town where Brooks's neighbors were the "quiet solid men of money," he had never been at home. Nor had his brother, Ames, who had solved the problem of displacement by placing himself as far as possible from Plainfield. "He walked in front of the early commuters' train one morning at the Plainfield station." Nor indeed had Brooks's father — a man of business, doomed to invalidism, yearning for

13

Europe — ever been at home in that suburb of Wall Street. "Had my father's practical failure in life over-affected my own mind, as his European associations had affected it also, so that perhaps his inability to adjust himself to existence at home had started my own European-American conflict?"

Although Brooks's thought tends often to lunge toward the pat answer, he did come to adulthood within a family in which Europe was represented as the solution for everything. But if his family proved anything it proved that Europe solved nothing. Eventually, believing that "deracination meant ruin," Brooks found himself impaled: "the American writer could neither stay *nor* go, — he had only two alternatives, the frying-pan and the fire." And Brooks made a self-conscious and brave choice: "the question was therefore how to change the whole texture of life at home so that writers and artists might develop there." All tremulous with misgiving he took on the truly formidable task, as Sherman Paul has observed, of making America Europe. Or, said in the terminology Brooks had devised, he would bring Ideal and Real, visionary imagination of the Germanic kind and cogency of systematic thought of the rationalist French sort, into a new and radically American balance. Returning to this country at a time of "Arctic loneliness for American writers," perhaps he would escape the wreckage his own family suffered.

This decision, a thing of high drama, was less momentous for American literature than the acolyte of art could have imagined and far more portentous for his inner life than he could have foreseen. Embracing a flimsy but plausible notion — deracination meant ruin — he returned to America almost in Puritanic renunciation of his deepest want. As is well known but ill understood, the scheme worked from 1914 when it was completed until 1925 when it and Brooks himself collapsed. In virtual casebook display of what Freud called the return of the repressed, Brooks in break-

down was haunted by the apparition of Henry James, by night-
mares in which James "turned great luminous menacing eyes
upon me." It was the figure of James that turned the screw of
nightmare in the late twenties. But many years earlier, in childhood, it had been not James but a Hindu who appeared in the
"earliest dream I remember," a "dream of flight." On the lawn
a Hindu suddenly appeared, dressed in a suit of many colors,
and chased the child Van Wyck with a knife. Just as he ap-
proached, running, "I soared into the air and floated away, free,
aloft and safe. On other occasions, the fiend was not an Oriental,
he was merely a nondescript minatory figure that pursued me,
and I was not even anxious when I saw him approaching, for I
knew I possessed the power to float away." That power — flight —
deserted Brooks during the years of crisis when his intricately
conceived scheme to evade wreckage was itself wrecked. And that
figure, neither Oriental nor nondescript but now a most elegant
avatar of deracination, of ruin, terrified Brooks with the minatory lesson: he who would evade himself is lost.

If this seems too fanciful a proposition, consider the trope to
which Brooks resorted in all moments of crisis throughout his
life, the image of seafaring, of journeying through troubled wa-
ters. It appears first in a pamphlet, *The Soul* (1910). "An Essay
toward a Point of View," it is composed of some forty gnomic,
Emersonian paragraphs on the transcendent subject, Art. The
genius of poetry, that "ancient companion of the human soul," is
its capacity to console: "in literature, I seemed to see a refuge."
Safe harbor too, literature, for a man to whom in fantasy human
existence appeared as a "vast ocean which contained all things
known and unknown . . . without a bottom." The lives of men,
"like so many ships," were "sailing, tacking, drifting across the
ocean. Some sailed swiftly . . . as if they steered for a distant
shore: but this ocean had no shore." Now and then a pilot would

drop a line into that bottomless sea and as it struck he "would take his bearings from this depth, supposing it to be the bottom. But this bottom was in reality, though he did not know it, only the wreckage of other ships floating near the surface." Then with a startling reversal of intent in what was conceived as a fantasy of consolation, Brooks says, "I will be this ocean: and if I have to be a ship I will be only a raft for the first wave to capsize and sink." That is to say, he would settle for nothing less than absolute literary triumph but he feared cataclysmic defeat.

Given this expectation of disaster, it is understandable that similar thoughts and images should have tortured him during that "time in the middle twenties when my own bubble burst . . . What had I been doing? I had only ploughed the sea." The wretchedness of those years is understated in Brooks's published reminiscence but the letters, especially certain exchanges between Mrs. Brooks and Lewis Mumford, record a state of sheerest horror all round. I must refer again to this unhappy matter, for it is a storehouse of images which connect Brooks's writings with the lower depths of Brooks's mind. Thoroughly "bedevilled," Brooks in print was later to say, he had seen himself as a "capsized ship with the passengers drowned underneath and the keel in the air. I could no longer sleep."

For five years he was unable to rest or work. Before then, from 1915 to 1925, he had achieved renown as the most metaphysical mind, the most urbane and eloquent voice, the most poised and coherent theorist of diverse movements in literary nationalism which flourished in the day of Resurgence. First with a group of pacifist, Wilsonian radicals on *The Seven Arts* — Bourne, Waldo Frank, Oppenheim, Paul Rosenfeld — and later as literary editor of Albert Jay Nock's paper, *The Freeman*, he acquired unparalleled authority among American intellectuals committed to one or another program of literary reform. Beginning in 1915 with

America's Coming-of-Age, he contrived to sail a brave course across the "Sargasso Sea" of American literary and social history, that "prodigious welter of unconscious life, swept by ground-swells of half-conscious emotion . . . an unchecked, uncharted, unorganized vitality like that of the first chaos." Then came *Letters and Leadership* in 1918, the noted essay introducing Bourne's posthumous *History of a Literary Radical* in 1920, and the last of these studies, "The Literary Life of America," which was published in Harold Stearns's symposium *Civilization in the United States* in 1921 and which prepared the way for the appearance of his climactic work, the book on Mark Twain. At mid-decade, barely forty, he had acquired national eminence as the leading spokesman for the Beloved Community, remorseless in his attack on a society which subverted the creative life in favor of the acquisitive life. Unlike H. L. Mencken, who chose the easy target of official Philistine culture, Brooks assailed his colleagues for having assisted at their own sacrifice. Jolted by and thankful for this shock of recognition, they had presented him with the Dial Award (for service to American letters) and offered him the editorship of that distinguished magazine. In print his many admirers expressed their gratitude for his labors in their behalf.

Brooks's fame represented a matchless moment of coalescence between the man and the epoch. His enterprise coincided with a general attack on the outrages of capitalism, with a rising labor movement, with an emerging Socialist party. Brooks, a socialist-pacifist who shared Woodrow Wilson's sense of mission, hoped to inspire, to exhort the American people to fulfill its destiny by presenting to the international community of nations a model of disinterested service to mankind. Simultaneously, he himself presented to the nation at large and to a special circle of rebel-intellectuals in small, a bill of particulars listing the reasons why Americans would be hard-pressed to realize Wilson's program.

Conflict within the national consciousness thus ran parallel to a polarity of will within Brooks's own consciousness.

As he wrote those works which, as Mary Colum said, helped to create "the conditions in which the artist can work and flourish as a free spirit," he discovered in classic American letters "two main currents running side by side but rarely mingling." In America "human nature itself exists on two irreconcilable planes"; its poetry, deprived of organic life, is therefore denied the right to fulfill its true office. In contrast to Europe, where art is the source of rapture and where artists mediate between the material and the spiritual life of man, Americans prefer the state of rupture. Two kinds of public, "the cultivated public and the business public," pursue divergent tastes which perpetually widen the gulf that separates them. The highbrow public exists on the plane of "stark intellectuality" and the lowbrow public exists on the plane of "stark business," of flag-waving and money-grabbing. Under these conditions poetry cannot harness thought and action, cannot transform the great American experiment "into a disinterested adventure." Brooks, having come this distance by way of his customary route — the language of dualism — ended his essay *Letters and Leadership* with his characteristic imagery. "So becalmed as we are on a rolling sea, flapping and fluttering, hesitating and veering about, oppressed with a faint nausea, is it strange that we have turned mutinous?"

In *Three Essays on America* (1934), he would seek to prepare the way for a guild of artists, men of "exalted soul" who would fuse the life of poetry with the life of action so that America, unified at last, would realize its old dream of utopia. But before this program of salvation could be properly carried forward, its theory wanted testing. And Brooks conceived a trilogy of books on classic American writers, Mark Twain and Henry James and Whitman, which would exhibit the full effects of all those patterns of disjunction — of wine and the aroma of wine, of French temper and German, of rhetoric and poetry, of Real and Ideal, of lowbrow and highbrow — he had traced during more than a decade's study. The books on Mark Twain and James would exhibit the consequences of lowbrow debasement and highbrow attenuation of spirit in American literature. And a final book would present Whitman as the very model of a perfect poet, a very Antaeus of a man who "for the first time, gave us the sense of something organic in American life." Brooks substituted Emerson for Whitman, so the story goes, when he learned of Whitman's homosexuality. On hearing this at lunch with Malcolm Cowley in the Harvard Club he left the table immediately.

However that may be, the revised project was greeted by members of his circle as the proper work of a man whose learning and eloquence were more than equal to the labor of representing what was then called the Young Generation in its debate with received opinion. And indeed by 1925 Brooks had discredited a whole tribe of university scholars who conducted literary affairs according to laws of taste which excluded the new criticism, the new poetry, the new painting — the new age. Reading Stuart Pratt Sherman on Mark Twain, Bourne told Brooks in a letter (March 1917), "made me chortle with joy at the thought of how much you are going to show him when you get started. You simply have no competition." Sherman "hasn't an idea in the world that Mark Twain was anything more than a hearty, healthy vulgarian . . . But you will change all that when you get started." Stuart Sherman, Irving Babbitt, Paul Elmer More — these were the men whom Edmund Wilson listed high among those Brooks cast out of authority.

The book with which he most outraged that older generation was *The Ordeal of Mark Twain*. Despite the fury this work roused among ritual cultists of Clemens, the *Ordeal* remains a compelling book. Securely placed among specialist studies of Mark Twain, it has an even more imposing place among bench-mark books in another kind of literature. For all its humorless-ness, its ax-grinding and thesis-mongering, the *Ordeal* bore some marvelous first fruits of inquiry into the connections between neurosis and art, unconscious motive and literary act. And par-ticularly as it raised some radical questions about the discontents of civilization in the United States, questions which its chief critic Bernard De Voto failed to discredit, has it earned its fame and proved its worth.

Mark Twain was no frontiersman of American jollity, Brooks argued, but was deep down afflicted by a "malady of the soul, a malady common to many Americans." His "unconscious desire was to be an artist; but this implied an assertion of individuality that was a sin in the eyes of his mother and a shame in the eyes of society." In fact the "mere assertion of individuality" was a menace to the integrity of "the herd," incarnate in that mother who "wanted him to be a businessman." This "eternal dilemma of every American writer" Mark Twain solved by choosing the mode of comedy even though he felt that as a humorist he was "selling rather than fulfilling his soul." His "original uncon-scious motive" for surrendering his creative life had been an oath, taken at his father's deathbed, to succeed in business in or-der to please his mother, Jane Clemens. This first surrender had been followed by another, to his wife Olivia, who imposed on her "shorn Samson" the prissy rules, sterile tastes, and vacant in-telligence of the genteel tradition. Until then surrender had been half- not whole-hearted. But when he married Olivia his life took permanent shape. Mark Twain, as his somnambulism indicates, became a "dual personality."

Somnambulism, gloom, obsession with double identity — these represent the effects of a "repressed creative instinct" which it is "death to hide." Repressed, Mark Twain's "wish to be an artist" was supplanted by another less agreeable but inexpungible want: to win public approval and acquire great wealth by conforming to public opinion. The impulse to conform clashed with the impulse to resist. This struggle, which implicated two competing wishes or "groups of wishes," undermined the genius of a man in whom "the poet, the artist, the individual" barely managed to survive. Because the poet lived on in cap and bells, the man managed to maintain a small measure of self-respect, to acquire high accolade and vast fortune, and preserve balance enough to outlast the despair which almost overcame him in the end. "I disseminate my true views," Mark Twain said in 1900, "by means of a series of apparently humorous and mendacious stories." The remark is given in Justin Kaplan's biography, *Mr. Clemens and Mark Twain* (1966), and Mr. Kaplan adds that at this time in Mark Twain's life "fiction, dreams, and lies had become confused, and he could not tell them apart. They were all 'frankly and hysterically insane.'" Mr. Kaplan's is a fine book, incidentally, which dispenses both with Freud and, unnecessarily, with Brooks — even as it takes up, amplifies, modifies the thread of Brooks's thought. What was hastily argued in 1920 is pursued at leisurely pace in 1966: *Mr. Clemens and Mark Twain* ends with the old man at the instant before his final coma talking about "Jekyll and Hyde and dual personality."

On publication, *The Ordeal of Mark Twain* split its readers into two camps which engaged in guerrilla warfare until Bernard De Voto in 1932, the year Brooks published a revised edition, offered in rebuttal *Mark Twain's America*. Accusing Brooks of having initiated a "fatally easy method of interpreting history," De Voto condemned him for incompetence in psychoanalysis, for "shifting offhand from Freud to Adler to Jung as each of them served his purpose" and (I refer to Stanley Edgar Hyman's view

21

of the affair) for "contradictions, distortions, misrepresentations, and unwarranted assumptions on page after page." Following De Voto nearly two generations of critics have taken up the debate. And in consequence today neither Brooks's wholesale derogation of Mark Twain's genius nor De Voto's wholesale condemnation of Brooks's thesis is quite acceptable.

Brooks's 1932 revision of the *Ordeal*, itself a product of his own years of desperation, represents a retreat from some hard-won positions. Far more ground was given up than is accounted for in a simple arithmetic of words changed or phrases dropped. This particular matter, comparison of texts, has been amply studied and I shall not reproduce details. It is true, however, that the ground he conceded was easily surrendered, and its loss did not appease those of his critics who admired the shape of his thought, as Gamaliel Bradford said in a letter (June 1923), but were distressed by the way he had used Mark Twain as a mannequin to hang a garment on. Brooks's tendency was to falsify — just a trifle maybe, Bradford agreed, but a trifle all the same. Brooks responded with an apology and a promise: he was very keenly aware of his evil tendency to impose a thesis on an individual. He agreed that the *Mark Twain* suffered from this, but promised that the *Henry James* would not, even if he had to spend two more years on the book.

The Pilgrimage of Henry James was to be an exercise in many kinds of self-discipline but it would confirm not correct iniquity. Brooks wrote both books in barely muted stridency of distaste for America, in an unrecognized and unwelcome ecstasy of longing for Europe. But the *Ordeal* was irretrievable for another, plainer reason: Brooks had lifted its skeleton from Hart's book on insanity. He was therefore flatly unable to accomplish the sort of radical revision which friendly critics would have admired. And since he chose not to identify Hart as his source of psychological learning, he left his critics to make out, with good guess and bad, the origins and ends of his thought. "Like the Freudians," Alfred Kazin remarked, "Brooks was writing to a thesis; but it was not a Freudian thesis." Nor was it an idiosyncratic pastiche, as other critics complained. It was Hart's composite portrait of the life of the psyche, Hart's synthesis of four schools of psychological thought — Freud's, Janet's, Adler's, Jung's — which Brooks adapted to his study of Mark Twain's psychic life. And it could not be jettisoned.

I have already remarked on Hart's contribution to Brooks's understanding of psychology. But this does inadequate justice to the tightness of connection which binds *The Ordeal of Mark Twain* to *The Psychology of Insanity*. Here is one of those rare and fortuitous instances in the history of ideas when direct and presiding influence, one work on another, is incontrovertible. Reading Hart today, you can recapture a measure of the excitement Brooks must have felt as he found in this handbook the key which unlocked the riddle of Mark Twain's life, of the creative life in America. In Hart's two chapters on "Repression" and "Manifestations of Repressed Complexes," he learned all the Freudian theory he needed in order to understand the principle of unconscious conflict. And in Hart's chapter on Janet, on "Dissociation," Brooks was given a ready-made system and language which accounted for some hitherto unaccountable traits of Mark Twain's character. The conception of dissociation enables us to represent the mental state of those patients, Hart said, whose delusions are impervious to facts. "They pursue their courses in logic-tight compartments, as it were, separated by barriers through which no connecting thought or reasoning is permitted to pass." One main form of dissociation was somnambulism; another was the commonly known one of "double personality." Illustrating the origins of somnambulism, Hart used an example offered by Janet: Irène, a young woman whose mother's death had been peculiarly painful, developed "an abnormal mental condition" whose symptoms resembled "those exhibited by the ordinary sleepwalker." Irène "would live through the deathbed scene again and again, her whole mind absorbed in the phantasy . . . oblivious of what was actually taking place around her."

What a thrill of recognition Brooks must have felt as he sorted out Hart's ideas, then reshaped Hart's pattern to match the design of Mark Twain's life and art. Retelling Albert Bigelow Paine's version of the deathbed oath — to which Brooks clung even though Paine's account, relying as it did solely on Mark Twain's recollections, was an undependable report of what Mark Twain chose to remember or misremember — Brooks let out the stops. "That night — it was after the funeral — his tendency to somnambulism manifested itself." It is "perfectly evident what happened to Mark Twain at this moment: he became, and his immediate manifestation of somnambulism is the proof of it, a dual personality." Now that psychology has made us "familiar with the principle of the 'water-tight compartment,' " we realize that Mark Twain was the "chronic victim of a mode of life that placed him bodily and morally in one situation after another where, in order to survive he had to violate the law of his own spirit." Having submitted to his mother's will, he assumed the character and attitudes of a "money-making, wire-pulling Philistine," a "dissociated self" which was permanently at odds with his "true individuality."

In explanation of the reasons for Mark Twain's submission, Brooks relied on Hart's paraphrase of ideas drawn from another prestigious work of the time, W. Trotter's *The Instincts of the Herd in Peace and War*. Trotter demonstrates the existence of a fourth instinct, Hart said, "of fundamental importance in the psychology of gregarious animals," a herd instinct which "ensures that the behaviour of the individual shall be in harmony with that of the community as a whole. Owing to its action each individual tends to accept without question the beliefs which are current in his class, and to carry out with unthinking obedience the rules of conduct upon which the herd has set its sanction." In "these struggles between the primary instincts and the beliefs and codes enforced by the operation of the herd instinct, we have a fertile field for mental conflict." What Trotter called herd Freud called superego. But Hart preferred Trotter to Freud on this subject, and Brooks followed Hart. Repression of Mark Twain's creative instinct was accompanied by the rise "to the highest degree" of his "acquisitive instinct, the race instinct." His individuality sacrifices itself, "loses itself in the herd," and in the end becomes the supreme victim of that epoch in American history, the pioneer, when "one was required not merely to forgo one's individual tastes and beliefs and ideas but positively cry up the beliefs and tastes of the herd."

Obviously Brooks's thesis was neither Freudian nor a pastiche of Freud and anyone else. *The Psychology of Insanity* provided a system of ideas on individual and social behavior which Brooks absorbed, paraphrased, and exploited in his programmatic study of both Mark Twain and Henry James. It was a matter of lock, stock, and barrel. To have tampered with this system would have been to dismember Hart's thought. Revising the *Ordeal*, Brooks could correct a howler or two, tone down or play up: pure cosmetics.

Revision of that book was his last sustained essay in the psychology of literature. A few years earlier, attempting to carry on with his projected three-book series of standard American authors, he had applied the techniques of psychology to the biography of Henry James — a work which he looked upon as a Purgatorio, following the Inferno of Mark Twain and preceding the

Paradiso of Whitman: strange fruit of the Harvard cult of Dante. In *The Pilgrimage of Henry James*, he had incorporated other aims as well. He had intended to examine the validity of James's view that the artist cannot thrive in the American air — an intention which he took very seriously indeed. For in this way, as he described the project to Bradford, he would rescue James from the Jacobites and show that James spoke the sober truth about the "immense fascination of England (applied to himself, that is, and in consequence of certain weaknesses in his own nature)."

In order to rescue James, Brooks was compelled to show that the great man, confronting frying-pan and fire, had deliberately chosen the frying-pan, Europe. The choice had been a bad one but James's judgment of the fire's heat had been accurate indeed. For James was "the first novelist in the distinctively American line of our day: the first to challenge the herd-instinct." Unlike Brooks, who immersed himself in the primitive American community, who fought it out with the "herd" — James fled. Flying, he "lost the basis of a novelist's life." He laid down a siege of London, won the war, lost himself. English society cut him "in two" and the public Henry James emerged, a "vast arachnid of art, pouncing upon the tiny air-blown particle and wrapping it round and round." Like Amiel, James spun large circles around the tiniest molecules of nuance. This was the James adored by the Jacobites, the Old Pretender whose play of style, a "mind working in the void," represented the ruin of art. Tracing ruin to James's deracination, Brooks concluded that a writer without a country of his own must sink in "the dividing sea."

Mark Twain the infernal lowbrow and James the expurgated highbrow were victims of a civilization which it was Brooks's holy mission to reform. This was all the truth he cared about, his Dantesque vision of America. Perhaps, too, the study of

James was intended to serve as a lesson in self-admonition at the very moment in the twenties when the fascination of Europe was irresistible to nearly all Americans. Having denied himself that refuge, Brooks had chosen literature as his safe harbor. But suddenly, shortly after he published this book, his ship capsized. And during the next five years as Eleanor Brooks and Lewis Mumford consulted physicians, enlisted friends, desperate for an effective way to restore Brooks to himself, he went from asylum to asylum in search of extinction, haunted by Henry James.

Until this time of crisis he had said marvelous things about the nature of conflict within the social and literary imagination. Out of his divided mind had come a new and stirring — though hyperbolic — account of polarity in the national experience. He had invented an ingenious vocabulary of antithesis, had analyzed diverse forms of dualism in England, on the Continent, and in America where, at last, he addressed to the Young Generation a full-fledged psychology, sociology, and philosophy of literary reform. A guild of evangels, these men and women would create a poetics of the body politic which would harness art and action.

Out of duality, singleness; out of diversity, unity: out of unity, wholeness; out of organic wholeness, order; out of order, utopia — this sequence of ideas served as the theme of Brooks's rhetoric until 1925. One fixed idea suffused the lot. Drawn from German and English Romanticism, it proclaimed that the creative life, the life of art, the artist's stubborn instinct for self-realization — "self-effectuation," Brooks said — must inspire individual beings to resist the herd. In this way the artist in America, Emerson's Orphic poet incarnate, would furnish all mankind with an exemplary figure of obstinate honor and untrammeled will.

Brooks's timing could not have been worse. He arrived at this stage of thought at the moment least auspicious for its exaltation. War had killed *The Seven Arts*; strain of will and gloom of spirit along with influenza had killed Randolph Bourne. And it was at this grim time of general disillusion that Brooks, completing his allegory, found himself at a loss. Unable to visualize that heaven which his prophecy had forecast, he was left with rhetoric alone. In 1925, when anybody in his right mind could see that an artist could really thrive virtually anywhere outside the United States, Brooks found himself utterly unable to contend that Emerson had prospered in an American atmosphere. Having proved that an artist is doomed if he stays here and damned if he leaves, having arbitrarily decided, for consistency's sake, that Emerson not Whitman would embody the triumph of American genius — having shifted from Whitman whom he adored to Emerson whom he had earlier half-reviled as dried manna of Concord — Brooks reached exactly that state of impasse he had observed in Symonds' life. First cul-de-sac, then breakdown. Having negotiated the Inferno and scaled Purgatorio, he found himself stalled at the gates of Paradise.

In the state of emotional collapse which followed we can discern some strange but telling conjunctions between Brooks's Dantesque allegory of the American soul, its progress from damnation to salvation, and Brooks's despair. In breakdown, his whole terror was fixed on the certainty of reprobation. Speaking with one of his closest friends, the scientist-adventurer-writer Hans Zinsser, whom Lewis Mumford brought East from California to consult and advise, Brooks tried to convince Zinsser that he, Brooks, was doomed to die of starvation in jail. In that panic time of guilt and self-accusation, he foresaw one sure end: punishment in hell. Much later, in autobiography, he was able to turn terror into a figure of speech, "Season in Hell," but in the late twenties he had no taste for conceit. What had begun as a term of rhetoric had become infernally real.

A man who accuses himself of crimes he does not commit must

surely be convinced he is condemned for some reason. When we remember that Brooks, a man of Puritanic conscience — "a conscience that was like a cancer," as he said in another connection — was terrorized by the apparition of Henry James, we cannot be far wrong if we guess that Brooks feared retribution induced by his "evil tendency" to falsify, to impose a thesis. And no advice could redeem regret or could assuage guilt or diminish the sense of evil. Mary Colum, for example, later told Brooks that in 1927 in Paris she had spoken with Janet — the theorist of dissociation — and Janet had said that Brooks's cure hinged on an end of meditation, of inquiry into the laws of his own inner being and into the inner nature of all other general laws of whatever kind. But he could scarcely disown overnight two decades of forensic, of meditation on the laws governing the creative life in Europe and America. Then too William A. White, another distinguished psychiatrist, gave contradictory advice. He told Mrs. Brooks that her husband should be encouraged to round out his work, should be urged to complete the book on Emerson. Indeed, apart from Janet, everyone was convinced that Brooks would be miraculously restored to health if only he could finish that third volume. If the Emerson succeeds, Mrs. Brooks wrote to Mumford, he will be cured. Only Brooks himself was unconvinced.

The problem he alone understood and could not resolve — whatever his physicians, wife, friends said — was not simply how to get on with Emerson but how in heaven's name could he speak of salvation when he felt himself cast out, condemned, disgraced. That this feeling was unreasonable is hardly worth saying: the strongest complaint that anyone could register against his work was that it was tendentious or, as Gorham Munson in 1925 maintained, that his kind of social and "genetic" criticism too often substituted moral fervor for formal analysis. But what drove him to distraction was loss of faith in his power of vision. The condition of life in America, he decided, was sheer hell from which there was no escape — neither in the classic American and paternal solution, flight to Europe, nor in immersion in private fancy. The only thing he could do was wait for the descent of that Hindu's knife, fit punishment for a faithless man.

And when *The Life of Emerson* (1932) did finally appear, it expressed no reassertion of faith but rather displayed Mrs. Brooks's, Mumford's, and the publisher's, Dutton's, faith in the healing power of love. This triumverate sought to do for Brooks what he was incapable of doing for himself — raise him from the slough of despond. Dutton accepted the manuscript, sent by Mrs. Brooks, on condition that Mumford take responsibility for the whole process, revision, proof, and the rest. Precisely how Mumford revised the manuscript is unclear. What is certain is that he performed this literary act with no less fidelity than he brought to bear on multitudinous other works of friendship during these hard years. For it was he who undertook to arrange for treatment by Jung, who assured Mrs. Brooks that money would not be permitted to interfere with therapy. His role in editing *The Life of Emerson* has not until now been generally known. Finding a splendid solution to this most delicate problem of literary tact, he carried out Brooks's intention to re-create the quality of Emerson's life by relying on Emerson's own words.

The season in hell ended shortly before *The Life of Emerson* appeared. Why it came to an end, what discoveries or disclosures eased his spirit, Brooks's autobiography does not reveal. Gossip says that private financial crisis had triggered Brooks's despair; and the end of crisis, in the early thirties, released him from despair. But I know of only one trace of confirmation for this view, Mrs. Brooks's remark to Mumford in 1940 about some problems of money: As usual she could say nothing to Van Wyck about this, she observed, for the mere sight of a bill temporarily destroyed his ability to write. Not really concerned to pry further — to go deeper is impossible and to speculate wider is unfair — I think the final word on the matter must be Brooks's own. "And even after I came back to life and sailed out clear and free I remained conscious at moments of an abyss beside me. I seemed to catch out of the tail of my eye a cold black draughty void, with a feeling that I stood on the brink of it in peril of my reason . . ."

On emerging from the abyss, Brooks foreswore allegory. But he did not forgo his intention to write an account of the "triumphantly successful literary life." Returning to the state of equipoise he set out, again tendentiously, to replace the life of Emerson with the whole "American pageant of genius." Having presented Emerson's life by way of stylized paraphrase of Emerson's own words, having found comfort in the state of anonymity which this style conferred, he embarked on a major effort of literary history, *Makers and Finders* (1936–55), which would "show the interaction of American letters and life," would connect "the literary present with the past," and would revive "the special kind of memory that fertilizes the living mind and gives it the sense of a base on which to build."

"May I say one further word about the method I have pursued," he was to comment in *The Writer in America* (1953). Responding to those critics who treated the five volumes of literary history as "a sort of irresponsible frolic or brainless joyride," Brooks described his method as that of a novelist whose every character, scene, and phrase were "founded on fact." But a more important word on method he left unsaid, its attribution to H. G. Wells whose habit of composition in 1914 he had cited and approved. "I make my beliefs as I want them," Wells wrote. "I make them thus and not thus exactly as an artist makes a picture . . . That does not mean I make them wantonly and re-gardless of fact." From Wells, Brooks learned to make brush strokes of the intuitive imagination which, he hoped, would lift the writing of history to the lofty realm of visionary art.

Beginning in the early thirties, Brooks engaged in a herculean labor of inquiry into the folklore and mythology of the creative spirit in all spheres of the American imagination from its origins until the present day. He described this project as a search for a usable past and his phrase stuck. Indeed, it is today no longer recognized as Brooks's phrase at all and seems to represent a peculiarly American attitude toward history itself, as is shown in recent volumes of historiography by Daniel Boorstin, *An American Primer*, and by Henry Steele Commager and Allen Nevins, *America: The Story of a Free People*. Strikingly, too, the kind of censure registered against these books is identical to that regis-tered against Brooks's *The Flowering of New England* on its ap-pearance in 1936. In accord with the doctrine of a usable past, "American history has invariably been written from Columbus to yesterday without the slightest change of pace or tone," we read in the *New Statesman* (June 2, 1967). The problem with this doctrine is that it contains within itself the idea of "the dis-posable past." Whatever does not fit goes to the scrapheap. It has "no place in your 1968 Model Past."

Reading *The Flowering of New England* and *New England: Indian Summer*, the first two volumes in *Makers and Finders*, René Wellek in 1942 mourned the disappearance of the old trenchancy of Brooks's mind, its replacement with a "belletristic skill of patching together quotations, drawing little miniatures, retelling anecdotes and describing costumes and faces." Still harsher criticism was uniform among a wide group of academic intellectuals which had been roused by Brooks's first books. "All my reading of American literature has been done during the era of Van Wyck Brooks and Parrington," F. O. Matthiessen said, but Brooks's new method of composition robs history of its clash and struggle and so dilutes the character of leading persons that it becomes hard to tell one man from another. However severe, these critics struggled to be just to the man who had revitalized their study of American themes. But even as they admired the very considerable merits of scholarship exhibited in these volumes, they condemned him for initiating that attitude toward history which today has apparently become stock-in-trade among our historians of a usable past. Brooks's nineteenth-century New England, F. W. Dupee remarked, "purged of conflict and contradiction," is presented as an "idyll of single-hearted effort." What was found unfit for this "fairy-tale" was disposed of.

The heart of the matter, as others have perceived, involves the interplay of proportion and distortion in Brooks's art. Although all writers must find external forms for internal states, must make their way through a labyrinth of motives, only a few are able to achieve an immersion in and conversion of but not subversion by their deepest wants. Brooks's myth-making embodied his inner life in vastly larger measure than it represented the exterior world, but until 1925 he contrived to transform the urgencies of private need into a prescription for society as a whole. Discovering in personal perplexity the key to a national dilemma, he defined some central confusions in American life and found for himself a short-lived relief from neurosis. In the early thirties, however, he wrote history with his eye on that cold black draughty void out of which he had so lately emerged. Our minds are darkest Africas, he told Granville Hicks in 1936, and he was at that moment exploring his own jungle trying to discover what he believed. Or, as he was to say in his sketch of Helen Keller, "She might have taken as her motto Theodore Roethke's line, 'I learn by going where I have to go.' "

Roethke's line could serve as his motto, surely, but could not justify the results of his explorations. Brooks himself maintained, in the books to which we turn now, those written during the last three decades of his life, that his early work had undervalued the American experience and that his later work merely restored balanced judgment to American studies. This position he staked out in the five volumes of history, the sketches of John Sloan (1955), Helen Keller (1956), and William Dean Howells (1959), the account of American expatriates in Italy, *Dream of Arcadia* (1958), as well as in the imposing array of works in self-explanation and self-justification: *Opinions of Oliver Allston* (1941), *The Writer in America* (1953), *From a Writer's Notebook* (1958), the three volumes of autobiography published intermittently from 1954 to 1961.

Makers and Finders, the chief ornament of Brooks's second career, is both a splendid achievement and a pernicious work. "Our greatest sustained work of literary scholarship," Malcolm Cowley has said, it has also been responsible for that view of the past which claims that authentic American literature avoids extremes, is neither highbrow nor lowbrow, but draws its inspiration from a will to resolve antithesis, banish contradiction. This view leads to the celebration of a style of literary culture, middlebrow, in which contrarieties are denied. It is a view, too, which bolsters an ideal of social order, in the style of President Johnson, where in the name of consensus radical conflict is ignored or suppressed. Above all it is a view which rests not on the history of ideas but on an illusion, a fable. And fables, as Descartes said in the *Discourse on Method*, "make one imagine many events possible which in reality are not so, and even the most accurate of histories, if they do not exactly misrepresent or exaggerate the value of things in order to tender them more worthy of being read, at least omit in them all the circumstances which are barest

34

and least notable." Those persons who hope to regulate their conduct by examples derived from such a source are "liable to fall into the extravagances of the knights-errant of Romance, and form projects beyond their power of performance."

Makers and Finders memorializes Brooks's decision to transform himself into a knight-errant of this order. Determined to avoid Mark Twain's situation or James's fate, he divorced himself from the immediate concerns of his day and turned his curiosity on the practices of earlier centuries. He expatriated himself not to England but to Old New England, that golden land where no base circumstance undermined the conduct of life.

The key to Brooks's failure as a historian is contained in a remark addressed to Cowley (October 1939): "For there is an American grain, and I wish to live with it, and I will not live against it knowingly." Adopting William Carlos Williams' phrase, he decided that this figure of speech, taken literally, would enable him to discover exactly what was "organic" in the American past. Whatever else must be said of this doctrine it can be seriously faulted as an example of what the medievalist Johan Huizinga called historical anthropomorphism and defined as "the tendency to attribute to an abstract notion behavior and attitudes implying human consciousness." This tendency, Huizinga noted, leads all too smoothly to another, to a reliance on the resources of figurative speech — metaphor, personification, allegory. Whenever "historical presentation is fraught with passion, whether political, social, religious," figurative language shades into myth and dispatches all hope of science. And if "beneath the metaphors the claim somehow remains that the figure of speech is still to be taken philosophically and scientifically," then indeed is anthropomorphism a subversive act of the mind.

Although Huizinga in this essay ("Historical Conceptualization," 1934) doubtless intended these reflections to bear on the problem of writing history in that day of ideology, fascist and communist, his thought illumines the problem of Brooks's ideology, too, the ideology of the American grain. Brooks, who was himself alert to the dangers of his position, wrote into the *Opinions of Oliver Allston* a crucial chapter, "A Philosophical Interlude," designed to circumvent judgments of this kind. As figures of authority he chose a heterodox group of system-makers — Croce, Thoreau, William James, Spengler — and drew from each what it suited him to have. Croce it was who led him to understand that America was "idealistic in its grain and essence" and that "the American mind was saturated with a sense of 'that which has to be,' — again in Croce's words, as opposed to 'that which is.' " If this view was considered unscientific, as Brooks anticipated his critics saying, so much the worse for science which is after all a discipline of thought not a guarantor of wisdom. Besides, he could make no "headway with abstract thinking, and, feeling that life was short, he abandoned himself to his tastes. To justify himself again, he copied out a passage from Thoreau's Journals (Vol. V): 'It is essential that a man confine himself to pursuits . . . which lie next to and conduce to his life, which do not go against the grain, either of his will or his imagination. . . . Dwell as near as possible to the channel in which your life flows.' "

Thoreau's view is unexceptionable. But nothing he said could justify Brooks's conviction that a peculiar socialismus of art and politics was apple pie but that "the communist mind runs counter to the American grain." This assertion occurs in the chapter on socialism in *Oliver Allston* where Brooks commended Williams for his fine phrase, then repeated the sentence from his letter to Cowley, and propelled himself headlong into the task of devising a whole new vocabulary of terms generated by the talismanic word, grain, itself. Thus reified, endowed with independent and objective life, the word conferred on Brooks's criticism the authority of pure American speech.

Expanding its range to include an infinitude of reference, he went to the language of psychotherapy for his formula of praise and blame. Having introduced Hart's language into the study of Mark Twain's life, he now concentrated his fire on the "Elioteers." To be always in reaction was "juvenile or adolescent" — were not, therefore, Eliot and Pound and Joyce infantile, sick, immature? "Were they not really unequal to life," these naysayers? Had not these very influential men of letters "lost a sense of the distinction between primary literature and coterie literature — was it not time to make this distinction clear?" Like primary instinct, "primary literature somehow follows the biological grain," he said, defining the exact "centre of his thought." Primary literature "favours what psychologists call the 'life-drive.'" The only value of coterie literature was its shock value which, like "insulin treatment for schizophrenia," restores the mind to its primitive state, a state of readiness for the fresh start. This treatment, coterie literature, is hardly necessary in America where the primary virtues of courage, justice, mercy, honor, and love represent the "tap-root" of art and "the sum of literary wisdom." To live in harmony with the American grain, in short, was to ally oneself with the forces of eros and set oneself in resolute opposition to the forces of thanatos, to the vanguard, coterie-writers, "children sucking their thumbs," who incarnate "the 'death-drive' more than the 'life-drive.'"

His opinions helped to confirm an opposition to modern literature in that new audience which read *The Flowering of New England* and *New England: Indian Summer* and presented Van Wyck Brooks with its highest awards. No longer addressing himself to the Young Generation of literary men, Brooks became a hero of middle-aged and middlebrow culture — became, as the *Partisan Review* said, a pilgrim to Philistia. All too comfortably, his former colleagues felt, Brooks slipped into the role of spokesman for a public to which modernist literary forms were impenetrable. All too easily, many former allies thought, he assumed the role of laureate of American chauvinism. Mary Colum, whose essay in 1924 had described Brooks as a pathfinder, a contributor of transforming ideas, spoke for nearly all his former colleagues when she told him in a letter two decades later that nothing he wrote about modern art showed that he knew what he was talking about.

There was in truth nothing in modern writing that Brooks cared anything for. What he did care about was to flush and dispel once and for all the issue of expatriation. He confessed that in his youth he had been "morbid" about this matter, that he had been "drawn to Europe over-much," that "many years had passed before he had learned to love his country," before he had realized that "he must cling to America to preserve his personality from disintegration" — and these extraordinary confessions explain the reasons for the conversion of Van Wyck Brooks and signify which motives underlay his fable. Along with the first two, the remaining three books in the series — *The World of Washington Irving* (1944), *The Times of Melville and Whitman* (1947), *The Confident Years* (1952) — result of nearly twenty years of independent research, supported only now and then by a grant-in-aid, form a national archives of forgotten documents, misplaced books, lost lives. Reading everything he could find lest anything of the least interest be neglected, Brooks restored to general view enormous numbers of hitherto ghostly figures. And if it were possible to set aside the fable, to take these five books as a movable feast of the American imagination, *Makers and Finders* would represent an absolute triumph of humane learning. If Brooks had had no larger aim than to revive a sort of racial memory among American readers and writers, there would be universal agreement to Cowley's view: these books caused "a revolutionary change in our judgment of the American past" and a "radical change in our vision of the future."

But it is impossible to set aside either the ideology of the American grain or the allegory of a usable past. How, for example, can we square Brooks's remark in a letter of 1933 — "I wish we could have in America the guild-life that writers have in England" — with the remark, made exactly two decades later in the essay "Makers and Finders" (*The Writer in America*) in which Brooks set down his final thoughts on his study of American history: "It seemed to me that . . . our writers formed a guild, that they had even worked for a common end." Presumably it was twenty years' research into the usable past which had led him to a major discovery. A reader making his way through the five volumes, however, is nonplussed trying to retrace the ground of Brooks's discoveries, trying to learn where Brooks had located this guild-life of American writers. Apart from a modest measure of support for this notion as applied to Boston during its heyday, the whole drift of evidence contradicts Brooks's point. Here are some examples taken nearly at random from *The Times of Melville and Whitman*: For nineteen years in New York, Melville was "all but forgotten as a man of letters." And Whitman — "to the end of his life the great magazines excluded him." After the first "flurry of interest on the part of Emerson and the dead Thoreau, he had for years only a handful of readers." Undoubtedly Whitman was "warped" by this treatment, Brooks says. Mark Twain, too, was warped by his conviction that American writers were merely "manacled servants of the public" — as if Walt Whitman "had never existed or Emerson or the free Thoreau or Cooper." Again, speaking of the main patterns of literary life in the seventies and eighties, when a few writers fled America, Brooks quotes Charles Godfrey Leland, whom in an earlier volume he had treated as a man with deep intellectual and emotional ties to his native Philadelphia: "I have nothing to keep me here. There is nothing to engage my ambitions."

Despite contentions made after the fact, Brooks was unable to prove that nineteenth-century American writers had indeed formed a guild. And in time he substituted another theme, the replacement of rural life with urban life. "More and more, as the eighties advanced and the cities grew larger and larger, the old life of the farm receded in the national mind." It was to this theme that Brooks committed himself without reserve. Deciding that the "immemorial rural life" had formed "the American point of view," he wove arabesques of history which were intended to show how a once "homogeneous people, living close to the soil, intensely religious, unconscious, unexpressed in art and letters, with a strong sense of home and fatherland" was uprooted and dispersed.

Determined at any cost to display the consistency of these ideas, Brooks engaged in exactly the kind of struggle he had recognized in Symonds, that "congested poet" who, upon recovery from breakdown, had assumed the "fretful activity" of a *vulgariseur* and had set down with great labor large works of scholarship which tried to do what "only poetry can do." I do not know, in 1934 he told M. A. De Wolfe Howe, "how to use my thousands of notes," but it was increasingly clear to him that he could not "think in the expository form." As he proceeded from book to book his vision clarified itself: he would re-create the dream of paradise. And there his fancy fled in order to preserve his mind against disintegration, against any relapse of despair. No matter how far he ranged, this aim remained

40

constant. Facts could not dislodge it though certain non-facts could be introduced to support it — the posthumous papers of Constance Rourke, for example (which he edited), or the phenomenal fact of Helen Keller's life.

Perhaps the most succinct way to crystallize the meaning of Brooks's double career is to note that the first half of his life was spent in demonstrating the ulcerous effects of America on the human spirit and that the second half was spent in an effort to prove that *America*, in its root meaning, signified the very spirit of health. Thus in 1956, publishing his sketch of Helen Keller, he sought to do justice to the biography of this marvelous woman and simultaneously to sanctify, by way of this inspirational tale, the whole design of his natural history of the American spirit. Was ever the physical life of man or woman more radically disfigured than Miss Keller's? Was ever the contour and lineament of moral health given more vivid configuration? She was "one of the world's wonders" — like Niagara Falls! He thought of Miss Keller when he read in Arthur Koestler's *The Age of Longing* that American women were too busy playing bridge to be cut out for the part of martyrs and saints. (Gladys Billings, Brooks's second wife — he had remarried in 1946, following Eleanor Brooks's death — was one of Henry Adams' "nieces," a figure out of Henry James.) Clearly Koestler had missed the point of America, had not got the point of James's *The Portrait of a Lady*, of Isabel Archer whom Miss Keller resembled in her "fixed determination to regard the world as a place of brightness, of free expansion, of irresistible action." Brooks repeated James's words in order to contend that Miss Keller's decision — "life was worth living only if one moved in the realm of light" — must be taken both as a personal victory and an American conquest, a triumph of private will and of national buoyancy, vitality. Didact to the end, he was convinced that the spirit's health was confirmed by those

41

powers of "affirmative vision" inherent within the unconscious American "collective literary mind" which, as revealed in *Makers and Finders*, enables us to revere, promote, maintain, renew our "dream of Utopia."

Two years before his death in 1963, admitting that he was known mainly as the author of *America's Coming-of-Age* and *The Ordeal of Mark Twain*, he confessed that his chief hope for some kind of relative permanence was in his historical series. We are tempted to ratify this hope. But when we draw together the main lines of belief on which his claims rest — when we realize that one way to take these five volumes, according to Morton and Lucia White's *The Intellectual and the City* (1962), is as "the most striking example of anti-urbanism" in contemporary popular thought — we cherish the brilliance but mourn the uses to which it has been put.

At the point of origin in American civilization, we can now say in paraphrase of his final position on this whole matter, a primary literature develops out of one of the two primary instincts of the unconscious, the life-drive. Serving as the source of high-mindedness in politics, it brought American national experience to fruition, united high art and heroic action, joined the cities and the plains during a century of national life. Then, in manifestation of cyclic laws governing all organisms, in conjunction with the decline of rural life, the death-drive acquired authority. And it in turn generated that coterie literature which accompanied the rise of great urban centers. Made of greed, fruit of thanatos, these deracinated modern cities brought catastrophe to birth out of the world's body. The last pages of the final volume, *The Confident Years*, present recent American history as a battleground between the forces of urban and the forces of rural life, a vision of apocalypse in which the "life-affirmers" engage in a battle of the books with the "life deniers." Wherever one "looked, in literature or in life, one found the two contrasting types," fighting it out as Brooks fought it out in unceasing battle with Eliot and the Elioteers. "So deeply engrained in the American mind" is life-affirmation, however, that the outcome was never in serious question. Because life-affirmation expresses the ineradicable will of the American spirit, it must eventually bring into being a new primary literature which will save the world from destroying itself.

Is it fair to say of all this, as he himself said of Symonds' achievement, that it was mere "high fantasy"? Had he composed book after book in praise of roots in order to devise for himself an utterly fanciful sanctuary? Is the figure of speech which he chose to describe Amiel and James an apt figure of self-description too: did he surround himself, spider-like, in a shelter spun from his own body? Had he labored to transform the ideas of expatriation and escape and flight into so sticky and labyrinthine a version of the American pastoral myth that only the most determined and powerful of Hindus could have found him out?

None of these is a fair question and all propose answers which are probably less true than false but are just true enough to record the fact that Brooks's unconscious life played a more intrusive and persuasive role in deciding the course of his career than was good for Brooks or for the history of ideas in our time. No essay in the psychology of motive, however, can deprive Brooks of his role as a leader of the new radicalism in American letters. And I am at a loss to understand why Christopher Lasch's good book on this subject, *The New Radicalism in America* (1965), takes up Bourne but utterly disregards Brooks. This lapse is the more startling in that Mr. Lasch's account of the radical tradition, very little modified, might stand as a virtual biography of Brooks's mind. At the outset, in 1900, reformers sought to see so-

ciety from the ground up "or at least from the inside out," Mr.
Lasch says. Eventually this new class of intellectuals came to dis-
trust the intellect, "to forsake the role of criticism and to identify
themselves with what they imagined to be the laws of historical
necessity and the working out of the popular will." Of this movement and process Brooks is indisputably the prime example.

Before he renounced the role of a radical critic, he imposed
his stamp on two generations of reformist literary men, on Mumford, Waldo Frank, Matthew Josephson, Granville Hicks, New-
ton Arvin — above all on F. O. Matthiessen whose *American
Renaissance* undertook to augment the Brooksian study of myth
with the techniques of formal, textual analysis. In this way, Matthiessen believed, American criticism might achieve the repos-
session of "all the resources of the hidden past in a timeless and
heroic present." As Matthiessen took up the subject where
Brooks left off, so too others carried forward certain main themes
of Brooks's thought which today receive cachet of the most flat-
tering kind in that these are no longer recorded as Brooks's
ideas at all but seem to express perennial wisdom. Reading a
series of axioms on American literature in *The Times Literary
Supplement* (July 20, 1967), we realize that the writer is unaware
that he has reproduced a configuration of ideas which goes back
fifty years to those first books in which Brooks examined our
"impulse toward literary cosmopolitanism" and explored the
"springs and sources of art and the right environment for its creation." It is this impulse "which has been of enormous importance in shaping the character of modern literature. Indeed it
has been of the greatest importance for western literature generally, since the very idea of modernism seems to have its roots
in this cosmopolitan, expatriate spirit." This matter of expatriation and cosmopolitanism has been of presiding importance in
modern writing not because some leading American writers have

been expatriates but because Brooks, obsessed by the problems of rootedness and deracination, their effect on the creative life in Europe and America, undertook to disclose the genesis of literature and discover the right environment for its creation.

This vast realm was once his private preserve. At the point when he turned his mind toward other problems, his friends tried to recall him to himself. "Do not, we beg you," Edmund Wilson addressed him in 1924, "lose too much the sense of that wonder," that excitement of the artist "enchanted by the spectacle of life." It was both good advice and bad. And in any event it came too late. For Brooks was already disabled by some critical side effects of a state of mind which the English writer Tony Tanner in *The Reign of Wonder* (1965) has found to be enlivening and debilitating in classic American literature. Mr. Tanner talks round Brooks but frames the general issue in ways which correlate his life with the lives of those great men of the nineteenth century, Emerson and Whitman and Mark Twain, who loom so large in Brooks's imagination. Like them, he was "too suspicious of analytical intellect, too disinclined to develop a complex reaction to society, too much given to extreme reactions, too hungry for metaphysics" to avoid what Brooks himself had recognized as an American malady, the malady of the Idea.

Surely it is time to install Brooks among his predecessors and peers, those American Romantics who traditionally have yearned to experience and to portray "the wholeness of the universe." The time has come to restore Brooks to the highest place among the most eminent of twentieth-century spokesmen of wonder in America.

⟋ Selected Bibliography

Principal Works of Van Wyck Brooks

The Wine of the Puritans: A Study of Present-Day America. London: Sisley's, 1908.

The Malady of the Ideal: Senancour, Maurice de Guérin, and Amiel. London: A. C. Fifield, 1913.

John Addington Symonds: A Biographical Study. London: Mitchell Kennerley, 1914.

The World of H. G. Wells. London: Mitchell Kennerley, 1914.

America's Coming-of-Age. New York: B. W. Huebsch, 1915.

Letters and Leadership. New York: B. W. Huebsch, 1918.

The Ordeal of Mark Twain. New York: Dutton, 1920.

History of a Literary Radical: Essays by Randolph Bourne, edited by Van Wyck Brooks. New York: B. W. Huebsch, 1920.

The Pilgrimage of Henry James. New York: Dutton, 1925.

The American Caravan, edited by Van Wyck Brooks, Alfred Kreymborg, Lewis Mumford, and Paul Rosenfeld. New York: Macauley Company, 1927.

Emerson and Others. New York: Dutton, 1927.

Sketches in Criticism. New York: Dutton, 1932.

The Life of Emerson. New York: Dutton, 1932.

The Journal of Gamaliel Bradford, 1883–1932, edited by Van Wyck Brooks. New York: Houghton, Mifflin, 1933.

Three Essays on America. New York: Dutton, 1934.

The Flowering of New England, 1815–1865. New York: Dutton, 1936.

New England: Indian Summer, 1865–1915. New York: Dutton, 1940.

Opinions of Oliver Allston. New York: Dutton, 1941.

Roots of American Culture and Other Essays by Constance Rourke, edited by Van Wyck Brooks. New York: Harcourt, Brace, 1942.

The World of Washington Irving. New York: Dutton, 1944.

The Times of Melville and Whitman. New York: Dutton, 1947.

A Chilmark Miscellany. New York: Dutton, 1948.

The Confident Years, 1885–1915. New York: Dutton, 1952.

The Writer in America. New York: Dutton, 1953.

Scenes and Portraits: Memories of Childhood and Youth. New York: Dutton, 1954.

John Sloan: A Painter's Life. New York: Dutton, 1955.

Helen Keller: Sketch for a Portrait. New York: Dutton, 1956.

Selected Bibliography

Days of the Phoenix: The Nineteen-Twenties I Remember. New York: Dutton, 1957.
Dream of Arcadia: American Writers and Artists in Italy, 1760–1915. New York: Dutton, 1958.
From a Writer's Notebook. New York: Dutton, 1958.
Howells: His Life and World. New York: Dutton, 1959.
From the Shadow of the Mountain: My Post-Meridian Years. New York: Dutton, 1961.
Fenollosa and His Circle, with Other Essays in Biography. New York: Dutton, 1962.
Writers at Work: The Paris Review Interviews, Second Series, introduction by Van Wyck Brooks. New York: Viking, 1963.

Studies in Criticism and Appreciation

Angoff, Charles. "Van Wyck Brooks and Our Critical Tradition," *Literary Review,* 7:27–35 (Autumn 1963).
Brooks, Gladys. *If Strangers Meet.* New York: Harcourt, Brace, and World, 1967.
Cargill, Oscar. "The Ordeal of Van Wyck Brooks," *College English,* 8:55–61 (November 1946).
Collins, Seward. "Criticism in America: The Origins of a Myth," *Bookman,* 71:241–56, 353–64 (June 1930).
Colum, Mary. "An American Critic: Van Wyck Brooks," *Dial,* 76:33–40 (January 1924).
Cowley, Malcolm. "Van Wyck Brooks: A Career in Retrospect," *Saturday Review,* 46:17–18, 38 (May 25, 1963).
Dupee, F. W. "The Americanism of Van Wyck Brooks," in William Phillips and Philip Rahv, eds., *The Partisan Reader.* New York: Dial Press, 1946.
Foerster, Norman. "The Literary Prophets," *Bookman,* 72:35–44 (September 1930).
Glicksberg, Charles I. "Van Wyck Brooks," *Sewanee Review,* 43:175–86 (April–June 1935).
Hyman, Stanley Edgar. "Van Wyck Brooks and Biographical Criticism," in *The Armed Vision.* New York: Knopf, 1948.
Jones, Howard M. "The Pilgrimage of Van Wyck Brooks," *Virginia Quarterly Review,* 8:439–42 (July 1932).
Kenton, Edna. "Henry James and Mr. Van Wyck Brooks," *Bookman,* 42:153–57 (October 1925).
Kohler, Dayton. "Van Wyck Brooks: Traditionally American," *College English,* 2:629–39 (April 1941).
Leary, Lewis. "Standing with Reluctant Feet," in *A Casebook on Mark Twain's Wound.* New York: Crowell, 1962.

Leavis, F. R. "The Americanness of American Literature," in *Anna Kerenina and Other Essays*. New York: Pantheon Books, 1967.

Maynard, Theodore. "Van Wyck Brooks," *Catholic World*, 140:412–21 (January 1935).

Munson, Gorham B. "Van Wyck Brooks: His Sphere and His Encroachments," *Dial*, 78:28–42 (January 1925).

Rosenfeld, Paul. "Van Wyck Brooks," *Port of New York*. New York: Harcourt, Brace, 1924; Urbana: University of Illinois Press, 1961.

Smith, Bernard. "Van Wyck Brooks," in Malcolm Cowley, ed., *After the Genteel Tradition*. New York: Norton, 1937; Carbondale: Southern Illinois University Press, 1964.

Wade, John D. "The Flowering of New England," *Southern Review*, 2:807–14 (Fall 1937).

Wellek, René. "Van Wyck Brooks and a National Literature," *American Prefaces*, 7:292–306 (Summer 1942).

Wescott, Glenway. "Van Wyck Brooks," *New York Times Book Review*, December 13, 1964, p. 2.

Wilson, Edmund. "Imaginary Conversations: Mr. F. Scott Fitzgerald and Mr. Van Wyck Brooks," *New Republic*, 38:249–54 (April 30, 1924). Reprinted in *The Shores of Light*. New York: Farrar, Straus, and Young, 1952.